How Angels Impact My Life

Shirlee Hall

inner child press, ltd.

Credits

Author
Shirlee Hall

Editor
Rhonda J. Ellis

Cover Graphics & Design
Inner Child Press
William S. Peters, Sr.

General Information

How Angels Impact My Life

Shirlee Hall

1st Edition: 2019

This Publishing is protected under Copyright Law as a "Collection". All rights for all submissions are retained by the individual author and or artist. No part of this publishing may be reproduced, transferred in any manner without the prior **WRITTEN CONSENT** of the "Material Owner" or its representative, Inner Child Press, ltd. Any such violation infringes upon the Creative and Intellectual Property of the Owner pursuant to International and Federal Copyright Law. Any queries pertaining to this "Collection" should be addressed to Publisher of Record.

Publisher Information
1st Edition: Inner Child Press:
intouch@innerchildpress.com
www.innerchildpress.com

This Collection is protected under U.S. and International Copyright Laws

Copyright © 2019: Shirlee Hall

ISBN-13: 978-1-970020-93-9 (Inner Child Press, Ltd.)

$ 12.95

Dedication

These true stories are for you. I know you are out there. No more hiding. We have found each other. Come fly with me.

Table of Contents

Introduction ix

Preface xi

Part I – Healing 1

Part II - Rescues 25

Part III - The Unexpected 43

Epilogue 69

about the Author 71
Other works by Shirlee Hall 73
Shirlee's Mission Statement 75
Web Links 77

This work of love is offered to God, our source, to the spirit of truth, to nature, and our angelic friends, without whom I could not have survived this amazing journey.

Introduction

Struggling souls need love. Angels assist us physically, emotionally, mentally and spiritually. When we cooperate with angels in the area of healing, we must understand that angels also desire for us to be balanced and free. On a soul or subconscious level, guilt may be lingering from past mistakes. Guilt and harsh judgments delay a complete healing. The angels understand and respect this fact and will not act against the higher will of the individual. A personal timetable or desire is not necessarily the right one according to the judgment of the soul. A healing may first require a strengthening of character, more respect for the body or mental adjustments in our thinking.

Some people are challenged with an affliction as an effect of a previous experience where harmful acts actually remain stuck on a subconscious level thus delaying the healing. Cause will eventually show up in life as effect. There are thousands of reasons for man's suffering. All causes are usually self-created. God does not punish us; we are the ones who have created disharmony and therefore, we subconsciously judge and punish ourselves.

Angels use touch, heat and light, dreams, visions and bursts of energy as their tools. As humans, we can lay our hands on other people and transmit healing magnetic energy from our body to the patient's body. Inviting the angels to participate in a healing exchange, in my opinion, increases the power many fold.

It is obvious, not everyone is helped. If this happens, do not condemn yourself. The action of divine intervention is very mysterious and rarely understood by the rational mind or emotions. A profound healing of the soul could have silently and secretly taken place and the individual not be conscious of the fact. Hardship is sometimes a tool used by the soul to awaken an individual to a higher truth and the experience of unconditional love.

You needn't belong to a particular religion or any religion at all to experience the angels or archangels. They are limitless nonphysical beings who typically help everyone who calls upon them. Think, write or speak their names and they will come. There are some who help and we are not aware of their presence. In other words, we do not have to do everything alone. Being involved in helping physical life regardless of its form is their purpose and joy.

Think of the angels as friends. All you need to do is be open to the idea, believe and be thankful. Archangels and angels can be summoned for earthly matters, attaining wisdom, helping with a soul transition, harmony, protection, healing, and other matters as mundane as a broken furnace.

Blessings of love and light,

Shi

Preface

If you are committed in your search for truth and have made a decision to love the journey, you will undoubtedly begin to have firsthand experiences with angels. Perhaps, you already have. Good! They are amazing companions whose love, light and wisdom enrich our lives immeasurably. Angels desire to share and assist in our spiritual growth, help us move more quickly to feeling very close to Source, our Creator, and are available to help us in times of great need. Their guidance and support are not to be taken for granted; it is something to rejoice in and to give thanks for.

Angels evolve as we do. They, too, have a spiritual body made of Light similar to ours although our true body is hiding behind the shell we are temporarily wearing. They usually appear as Light, a Light that is an emanation of Divine Love in action. They also may appear to look as humans. Angels are friends and not personal servants. Their purpose is service. Angels appear when Spirit wills. We can't force it, nor should we try. Humans who believe and trust frequently have angelic beings as active companions.

We often sense their presence and on special occasions actually see them through our awakened spiritual senses. In mythology and the sci-fi stories, the language used to describe the ability to witness the 'other side' is called prescience. A person is able to see everything both physical and nonphysical with his physical eyes either open or closed because he or she is actually seeing with a higher sense that does not rely on lights turned on or off. Spiritual sight is a divine one, a dormant talent in humans that may surface for our benefit at any time. Interestingly enough, animals have the ability to see the 'invisible' worlds not commonly observed by most modern day humans.

As we strengthen our connection with angels, the greater the help received. All over the world people have recorded thousands of remarkable encounters. Angels are designated for every type of situation. We are students and our celestial companions are powerful teachers we need to pay attention to by listening and observing with humility. The secret, besides a firm belief in divine assistance, is to establish a working relationship with your guardians during good times. When you find yourself in a position where you need help, reach out and they will come. What I have found through firsthand experience is they intuitively know before we do when we will be confronted with a challenge. Guidance may come through an unexpected Voice, visions, symbols, dreams and insights or a deliberate physical response.

My lifetime experiences with angels have been primarily with three different types: rescue, healing, and guiding. Angelic help is the science of a Divine Mind or Presence that loves us unconditionally. If you keep belief and mind and heart focused and strong, your request for help will be answered. Requirements include an acceptance and a sense of knowing that you are being heard. No contradictory thought or feeling is present, only an explicit inner trust that the job will be done. What amazes me is that often the angels take action before we actually call for help. They already know what will happen to us.

All life forms are involved in the spiritual evolution process. This includes the invisible worlds of Light and Love. Our helpers may remain unseen for the most part, but with increasing frequency they are allowing themselves to be visible to humanity. It is important for me to clarify what I mean by invisible beings. I am not referring to departed relatives, friends, or souls who have lived in physical bodies and desire to help. Nor am I referring to master souls who once lived in physical form. I am referring to a different form of intelligence and Light who are normally free from physical birth.

Angels obviously existed prior to human life. They are social creatures with responsibilities and personalities and a sense of purpose and organization. They serve God and help life as they, too, seek to live and grow perfectly in their special realms of Light.

For the purpose of this offering, the emphasis is on the angelic friends who help us in time of need. Our intent and success is noticed by the invisible worlds. Angels genuinely care about us. From the very beginning of creation, they were appointed as guardians to watch constantly over life regardless of the form that life takes until we evolve to a higher level of consciousness and energy.

With gratitude, love, and joy, may you receive the love that I am offering through select personal ongoing experiences that have instilled a powerful sense of hope, understanding, and purpose in my personal adventure.

Blessings of love and light,

Shi

Part I

Healing

How Angels Impact My Life

Service

A lifetime of healing successes with myself and others has provided the knowledge and experience to share these words. The examples described have occurred over the larger part of my life. Healing began in my own mind and body. A passionate desire to be free of any form of bondage and live as wholeness and truth became the measure for my life. The desire was to fully remember who I spiritually am and consciously reflect the Light. I was and still am determined to live by the One Power and Presence within and allow no thought, person or experience to deter me. I knew that with my healing I could help others heal themselves. Success attracts other souls.

Healing is about loving Self, the truth of your being. It is one of many ways to demonstrate understanding of what God is. You awaken to the joy of loving the truth of your own spiritual identity and the identities of others. You are like a scroll unfolding memory of a beauty and magnificence that is beyond words or finite understanding. You are love rediscovering a higher version of yourself.

To live and sustain a consciousness of healing in the midst of disorder and separation, you must be at attention and know with all your mind and heart what your lasting and higher identity is and accept the truth of an invisible and living spirit or light within. Yes, a perfect being lives within and you live within it. The only thing that separates is our sense of separation through false conditioning. Allow the perfect image to emerge in your mind and body. People generally invent a God according to their belief, so that God is the embodiment of man's belief. As our belief changes, so our God changes; but the true Source, One, never changes. Instead of worshipping in fear, we need to worship from love.

We begin to understand the Power and Presence of God within through healing. The Invisible becomes visible. Our inner nature is that same Power and that is where we are equal. Realizing, accepting and using the Power for good are up to us. God Realization in the body is the goal of the soul. Healing whether it is physical, emotional, or mental is part of the process of our remembering spiritual identity and becoming visibly, tangibly who we are in the objective world of the senses.

When we heal, we feel a higher love. We gain the intimacy of God, the real nature of who we are. Love is our power source. We attract to us what we believe. Freedom is the result of healing the soul, mind and body. All healing begins within. We can be healed in a moment. I have actively participated in thousands of those moments. The Spirit within desires a stable home. It requires harmony to be Its Self. God does not favor suffering, lack and limitation. The personality has temporarily forgotten the true inner Nature.

Healing occurs when we are conscious of perfection and unconscious of imperfection. Perfection is a natural law. No human can teach spirituality. We can be an example and share our own experiences. One of the ways we reveal God is through the power of healing. You can be a healer not only of yourself but a remarkable healer helping other people as well.

There is holiness, a sacred energy within. Focus on that energy and not opinions of others that have influenced you. We are a part of God. The more we understand and accept this reality, healing becomes a living reality.

The following question frequently comes up. Some people, good people, do everything 'right' and they still suffer. Why is this? The reasons are many and obviously differ in individual cases. The primary cause in not quickly healing is that there is something the individual has judged about his or her self that still needs adjustment. A hidden issue is causing the imbalance in the mind and body. More often than not, it is an opinion. They usually do not know the issue until that moment that they suddenly do. This is when the healing happens. It is far better that they learn the 'reason' firsthand than to be told the answer; it is more lasting and effective.

Sometimes, undergoing medical treatment is the best option and that choice actually becomes part of the learning experience and healing.

The main point I wish to stress in my story is that angels are present although you may not feel or see them. They are real beings of intelligent Light whose role is to serve and help when we believe and trust. There is so much wonder waiting to be discovered and enjoyed right here in our midst. Yes, we definitely have celestial friends who are here to help. I hope you enjoy meeting them as much as I do in having experienced their unlimited talents, beauty, quickness, and power.

Perhaps because of angels and their ability to do the magical without effort that we are as humans also fascinated with the superheroes depicted so fervently by modern culture. We want to believe that there is a 'living god or goddess' existing here on earth. A Super being with an ability to do what we regard as impossible often becomes a 'savior' because he or she is approachable.

Heroic figures give us hope. Some of us aspire to be like them. I like the idea that they usually inspire us to be better, to do the right thing and be selfless. Yes, they make mistakes, but continue with determination and courage. Many people have transferred their admiration from angels to superheroes, or they embrace both. We love superheroes because we can relate to them. As you listen to my true story about angels and read my published books, hope will be renewed and infinite possibilities return to your consciousness. An increased intimacy with the angelic kingdom will be an option for you to discover.

We enhance our energetic power when we embrace the magical. A higher intelligence and love is available to all of us when we consciously align with the angels. If you do not love them already, you will by the time you finish reading or listening to my message.

We also admire superheroes regardless of the form they assume. Secretly, we would like to be one as well. For many of us, they represent a standard to strive for, an ideal role model. The collective soul of humanity needs to rise up and accept the truth that we can save ourselves and that there are angels of light and love who have been nearby always willing to help us to become our true and magical identity. We already have the angelic or super nature within us. Let us together acknowledge this ancient truth and model our lives after their sublime example. Remember, angels are real and not make-believe and their nature is part of our nature although it is commonly hidden.

Surrender

I had lived a life filled with psychic and intuitive experiences as many people do, but something unexpected happened to change the more common into the extraordinary and beautiful. I experienced a higher love that could not be denied. I had given birth to my third child and while in the hospital another surgery was performed. I was home approximately three days when it became obvious that something very serious was happening in my body. The stitches from the selective surgery were highly infected, red streaks blazed across my abdomen, pain was constant, and I had a high fever.

It was 10:00 AM and I had just fed the baby. Alone in the house, I knew I should call an ambulance and have the infection taken care of. I didn't know what to do with the baby or who to call. I then made an unusual decision. Instead of calling for human help, I went back to bed and surrendered my life to God. I fell unconscious for one hour.

Upon awakening, I realized the pain was gone, my stomach flat again, the red streaks had disappeared and I did not feel feverish. As I moved my hands across my abdomen, I felt a sticky substance. All the infection had drained out spreading over my skin. A higher Presence, angels, had created an opening at each end of the five-inch-long stitches in order for the infection to be released. In joy and relief, I immediately got up and cleaned the area and covered it with a large bandage. It felt like I was born again as a result of having experienced celestial love. The blessing arrived unannounced and helped me in a very needed and important way. As the result of the healing, my life changed forever.

Teenager

When my children were in high school, one of them, including my niece, would invite troubled classmates to our home. Our young guests were looking for a way to feel better about themselves and life. They knew that in our home they would not be judged. Sometimes, a teenager would come hoping for a healing of a physical concern. A loving example of an angelic healing was a young girl who I had never met before unexpectedly sharing with me that she was scheduled for surgery on a growth behind her one eye. I knew nothing about her, including her health. She asked me to pray and lay hands on her. It was not until weeks later that her friend told me the wonderful results. It's funny in a way how people sometimes assume that I know everything. I don't. I call the angels and do what I do and release it. About a week later, I heard that the eye surgery had been cancelled, because an angel answered the call. The teenager believed that a healing would occur and it did. To be able to facilitate the healing of serious disorders, we must understand the action of God's Law of Love and apply the love with confidence.

Assistance

Angel assistance occurs on the 'other side' as well as here on Earth. There have been occasions when a departed soul will come forward and request that I pray for him. This has been true for suicides. A friend's neighbor asked her to contact me regarding strange activities occurring in the basement of his home. Both he and his dog no longer would go down the steps for any reason, because they felt 'something' was down there that was very disturbed.

When I visited his basement, I brought candles and sacred music to play in the background. The owner, his dog and my friend cautiously followed me downstairs. With candles lit and music softly playing and incense burning, I walked slowly around the basement. It did not take long before I became aware of a young man in his body of light desiring my help. He mentally told me that his parents didn't have a normal burial service for him, because he had committed suicide. He asked if I would create a service, so he could leave in peace.

As said, the candles were already lit, the incense burning and the music playing. I then conducted a simple service and called the angels for assistance. They came and surrounded the young man and escorted him upward and out of the house. What was so fascinating for the three of us who witnessed this act of love, was the current owner's dog whose head turned and watched the angels and the young man leave the premises. Animals are very aware of the finer dimensions.

Faith

One of my favorite experiences with healing involved an elderly woman. I was surprised to hear that she had experienced daily pain since seventeen years old. It turns out that her family would hire her out to work on neighbor's farms. I cannot recall the injuries that occurred to her and that is not the point. The point is she never complained, went on and married and gave birth to four children. I discovered her husband was an alcoholic and every family member was in fear of him. All this was learned after the healing. She was a new friend and I strongly felt she not only deserved a healing, but her faith would make her whole.

As I stood behind her with my hands on her head, the angels blessed me with a vision. I was shown one of this sweet and quiet woman's earlier nasty experiences. I immediately shared it with her. Apparently, having carried guilt for a very long time, she was continuing to punish herself. Instead of asking the angels to heal her, I made a very specific request to the woman as a direct result of a suggestion the Angel of

Faith gave me. I told her that if she accepted what I was going to share with her and forgave herself, a lifetime of physical and emotional pain would vanish. She would be free of physical suffering. I then said that I was going to leave her house and return home. All she was required to do is go into her bedroom and in solitude and silence forgive herself for the former ugly incident and she would be completely free of her normal daily pain. After I left, this is exactly what she did. She believed the angel's message, she trusted me, and what we often refer to as a miracle happened instantly.

Not only was she completely healed, the senior continued to live to the ripe age of 107 as a beautiful example to all of us of true faith. It is one thing to talk about faith; it is quite another to put it into action.

Vision

When I was a young mother of two children, I did quite a bit of night driving. I had noticed increasing difficulty with vision at night, a sensitivity to light and glare, and seeing 'halos' around street lights. I was used to seeing 'halos' through the spiritual senses around people, but seeing them at night around artificial lights was a huge distraction. Something was definitely not right. I finally took the time to have my eyes examined. The physician said that cataracts were forming in both eyes. This was a huge surprise, because I always associated cataracts with people who had already reached an 'advanced' age.

I called my mom and asked her if this could really be possible. She told me that she had a nineteen-year-old cousin who developed cataracts. Well, I didn't have time for this nonsense. I went and sat in my favorite meditation chair that night and called on the angels. My faith was so strong that I felt it would be a simple task for my 'higher' friends to take care of this inconvenient situation. One prayer and they were gone. I made an appointment to be examined again, because all symptoms had disappeared and I wanted medical verification. The eyes were in perfect health.

The secret to success is to ask, assume a higher Power and Presence is making 'the crooked places straight,' let it go, and be filled with gratitude, expectancy and love knowing that because of your faith what is best will occur. Somehow I had brought this understanding with me at physical birth. It has been a very strong part of my nature.

Archangel Raphael

A very special moment occurred unexpectedly one night. I was lying in bed having a difficult time falling asleep. I seem to do all my creative work mentally when the condo building is quiet. Suddenly, an enormous figure appeared by the side of the bed. Its appearance was so startling that I actually gave out a brief scream. The angelic being remained long enough for me to examine his appearance and ask a question. Who are you? He replied, "Raphael."

I associate the name Raphael with healing. Of course, probably like you, I Google/research everything right away. It turns out that he is known for healing and compassion for people who are struggling physically, mentally, emotionally, or spiritually. The part that really pleased me is his work healing animals and supporting environmental efforts on Earth. So, if that is one of your focuses, call on Raphael to help you.

Raphael means God head and Beauty on the Cabbala's Tree of Life. Since he is known as the angel of healing, it was an indication to me that it was time to reach deeper and heal any lingering wounds. Research told me, "Raphael feels partial to those in all healing professions and will in some way guide those individuals who are unsure about what directions to take for appropriate health care for their 'clients,' etc. If needed, he will offer ideas for speedy healing and assist in a medical crisis by getting together the perfect team to work together.'

Archangels are extremely loving and egoless. We don't need to belong to a particular religion for them to appear or help us. They also are like a manager overseeing guardian angels. There are many who help us whether we are aware of their presence or not. There is no way we can overburden them. The idea behind my sharing these stories is that we don't have to do everything alone. Being involved in the advancement of humankind is their purpose and joy.

Purpose

I was called to our local hospital to visit a stranger. Upon entering the room, I observed the visitors and family surrounding her. The woman in bed had pneumonia, was on oxygen and also had cancer. The first thing I asked her was, "Do you want to live?" She weakly responded yes. She had an adopted daughter who needed her. A good reason to live is very helpful in all healing. I mentally called the angels and immediately was given a vision. The vision was of the woman in the bed wearing a black print dress quickly moving through her daily activities.

I described the dress to the woman and she acknowledged that she owned a dress that fit the description. Then, I confidently told her that she would be well; I had seen her future. The husband called the next day and said that her temperature had returned to normal and she was taken off of oxygen immediately after I left. The stranger in the bed who totally trusted in the angelic message I shared with her went home soon afterwards.

Cooperation

A stranger came to a monthly class in my home, never informing me of any of his concerns. This was in a group setting and a close friend had invited the stranger to join us without mentioning why. At the end of our classes, we would put out chairs for people who were seeking a healing. The stranger silently sat down and I stood behind him. Knowing none of the particulars, I called on the angels. He sat quietly and never said a word even when leaving later in the evening.

A month passed and I had forgotten the visitor until at the next meeting I asked his mutual friend as to whatever happened to his guest? Our regular class member casually said to me that the gentleman's hearing had been corrected as a result of the healing session. In this particular case, it was a gradual improvement over several weeks. He also added that his friend had the faith and confidence that the angels did heal him. He kept offering gratitude for his perfect healing. Remember, preferably, a soul healing occurs first. An excellent cooperative effort between the 'patient' and the angel had led to the physical healing.

A Different Lens

I've been very myopic since junior high school and usually wore contact lenses. One day when I awakened I found I didn't need to wear the contacts. I could see perfectly. I did not ask for a healing; it just unexpectedly happened. Of course, I was delighted. I could actually see across the street from my living room window. Unbelievable! I never asked the angels why, because I grew up with unusual and unexpected experiences.

It so happened that I had a luncheon date that day. The plan was to meet my friend at a restaurant only five miles away. I obviously had to think seriously about the drive and being in control of a car with my eyes behaving so strangely. With my usual trust and confidence in the love of the Divine, I drove to the mall restaurant. Although my friend had already sat down at a table, I found her quite easily. The same held true for reading the menu and the drive home. The perfect vision lasted all day and suddenly vanished before I went to bed.

I don't believe I ever mentioned this to anybody, but I have done some Internet research and cannot find any reference to the possibility that someone who is very myopic can in one moment have their eyesight transformed and experience perfect vision that lasts all day and then suddenly reverts back to its former weakness. It makes me wonder if the experience could possibly be a very unusual way to demonstrate how humans see life through a very different lens than the angels view it. The lenses we see through are very cloudy from both a philosophical, spiritual and physical perspective. Perhaps, this was another way, although very dramatic, to teach me that there is a higher perspective where perfection exists. We simply need to be consciously aware of it and then live it.

A Mother's Love

A woman who had attended a couple of my classes called and asked if I would visit her teenage son in our local hospital. Tommy had been in a very serious automobile accident and was not expected to live. When I arrived at his room I waited, because a priest was standing over the young man administering the last rites. Tommy's mother and a woman friend were also standing by the bedside. Eventually, the priest and the two women left me alone to enter the room and be with a barely conscious boy. Later, they explained to me that they chose to leave the room, because they felt an electrical energy in their arms and hands, a very high vibration that was rather overwhelming coming from where I was standing. I refer to the energy as the Holy Spirit, creative power. The power is an energy that cooperates with the angels who were also present.

I was alone with the young man and didn't touch him...only prayed. He opened his eyes once and looked at me. After about fifteen minutes, I felt God's Work was completed. I left without saying a word to anyone. I rarely do. I have found through experience that miracles happen best in the Silence of God's love. The young man fully recovered. In fact, a couple weeks later on a beautiful sunny afternoon, he showed up unexpectedly at our home. Tommy looked amazingly healthy and handsome. I wish he had called ahead of time. Because he did not know what was going on at that moment behind closed doors, I did not invite him into the house. I am certain he came to say thank you. His appearance was in a way similar to an angelic visit for me to experience.

Animals

One of my first healing-angel experiences was with our family Siamese cat. Rama was always hissing and very skittish. I decided to take him to a doctor and get a professional opinion. After a careful examination, the doctor said Rama had been born deaf. I didn't expect that answer.

How Angels Impact My Life

I couldn't help but think how innocent animals usually are. They don't play the blame game nor do they usually feel guilty about a wrong action. If so, only briefly. Humans normally are mesmerized into the trap of feeling they are unworthy. Excuses are found to explain why they have a problem.

Viewing Rama as innocent of any past karma that would be the cause of his deafness, I decided to call on the angels. Why? Because I have always known that matter can be changed, it is a shell covering our light, our true body. I was born with a strong faith in the Divine. Freaky things sometimes happen to the innocent, so why not ask for help or cooperation in correcting them. What a doctor or human cannot do, the Holy Spirit and the angels can easily handle.

There is no set way of going about a healing. I can tell you that I am always confident, specific and then let the request go. Holding the cat, a prayer for healing was offered. My youngest son participated in Rama's transformation. After calling the angels, I requested that compassion and love take over. We both assumed Rama would hear perfectly for the first time. Within fifteen minutes, he had perfect hearing. How did we know this? We immediately ran a series of tests such as shaking house keys, playing hide and seek and using imagination in various ways to prove that we now had a cat with perfect hearing. Rama had never enjoyed playful activities before.

When you have a problem, regardless of what it is, reach higher, think properly, and know there is angelic help. Rama's hearing materialized. Isn't that genuine magic?

Magic is belief. If we can be part of that magic, anything can happen. Perfection replaced Rama's imperfect hearing. Can you imagine how happy our pet became? More humans could participate in genuine healings if they would remember their own spirituality and simply imagine. I definitely did not believe for a single minute that our Siamese cat needed to be deaf. Perhaps, more of us need to step out of fear and accept that there is angelic help.

I love animals. Baba, a combination Maine Coon and Manx cat is our current fur baby. He loves to meditate and intuitively knows when it is time for me to sit in a particular chair and participate in a remote healing. Many of my friends actually request that he participate in their treatment, which I feel is very special.

Animals are very psychic. They are able to see the subtle worlds of Light easily and it is usually very obvious when it happens.

Pain

We had invited friends and their son to spend the day with us and visit our city's end-of-the-summer festival. When they arrived, I was surprised to find the husband lying in the back seat of his car groaning. Although it was a long drive to our home and he was experiencing serious pain, there had to be a particular reason why he chose to suffer discomfort and still join us.

I asked him what was going on. Unbeknownst to me, he had for many years experienced sudden and very painful attacks in his spinal area. His wife told me that he had suffered greatly and it always occurred unannounced. His only partial relief was to lie down on the ground wherever he was until the attack finally left his body.

I squeezed into the back seat next to him. I quietly told him that his spine would be corrected. Calling on the angels, I laid my hands on him. The hands do not need to be on the area of distress, because the angels go past any so-called barriers. The angels knew what to do and his healing occurred faster than it is taking me to share this. He was so startled by the speed of the healing that had crippled him periodically over many years that he assumed I had hypnotized him. It was funny how he kept saying what did you do? You must have hypnotized me on and on.

I laughed and told him about the angels. As a practicing Jew, he knew about angels and his wife must have told him at one time about my working relationship with the angels.

He quickly got out of the car, walked happily into our home, and sat down at the dining room table where I had already laid out a spread for our enjoyment before leaving for the festivities.

In the years that followed, he never ever experienced that same horrific spinal pain again.

Unexpected

I will share one more healing story involving a stranger to me visiting his relative in my neighborhood. I did not know the neighbor and never asked how she got my name and telephone number. She called mentioning that her elderly uncle was visiting for the weekend and was very ill from inhaling a poisonous substance. Her uncle was to lead a Friday night and Saturday all-day workshop regarding the study of human consciousness.

I never found out his name until a few years later when I learned he was an American physician / scientist, author / lecturer and a leading pioneer in the study of the mind and healing. Ironically, he could not present his workshop because he collapsed and felt miserable. I remember it was night and the neighbor's home was already filled with people waiting to hear this man's views. As said before, much later I found out that he was famous and also had traveled all over the world, studying 'healers' for scientific purposes. In many ways, he was a man shrouded in mystery.

I was abruptly left alone with a man who looked very much like Albert Einstein. Lying on his back, he simply stared at me and I at him. Neither of us said a word but he intently watched me. Silently I called on the angels and did what came to me intuitively. After approximately fifteen minutes, I was finished. He sat up and reached over to a bedside table and picked up his watch and showed it to me. On the watch was the same creative energy symbol that I have worn hanging on a chain around my neck daily ever since a vision.

Nothing was said, but we smiled and he was totally healed. I later learned he immediately got up, went into the other room, gave his lecture, and continued in perfect health the following day when he offered a powerful workshop.

There are many more stories I could share. In my understanding, a true healing is mastery of self. It is our destiny. It is the rare soul who becomes the greatness that it actually is, here in matter due to erroneous human programming. The fact that you are taking the time to listen or read my experiences indicates that this is your moment. Are you ready to do the right work and reclaim your true spiritual identity by walking through the Front door leaving ignorance and suffering behind?

While we are in this stream of thought have you ever considered that disease is a belief and it is not self-existent, nor created by God, but is purely an invention of man? It is so firmly established in most people's beliefs that its authenticity is never questioned. Perhaps, if more of us would destroy the faith or belief in illness and not accept other people's opinions we could actually be free of disease.

What if disease is actually our creation? It is being proven over and over again that it is caused by a disturbance of the mind. It is in the mind where disease originates. Could it be that diseases are real to us through the result of belief? A simple example was a young mother that I knew who often said that she was going to die of cancer. I asked her why she believed that. She then rattled off how her mother, aunt, and others in her family died of cancer. She believed and it did happen leaving young children without a mother because of false programming. Just because a disorder 'runs' in the family doesn't mean you will inevitably get it yourself. Everything that happens to us is based on belief, what we hold in consciousness as our truth.

If we believe in something, eventually it will manifest. Our feelings are powerful. We need to give serious thought to the error of our thinking and ask whether we are actually deceiving ourselves, thus making an illness or tragedy into a reality that does not need to be. Remember to ask yourself when you feel ill if an opinion created the problem. I have found that anything unpleasant that appears in the body is a misguided thought we have accepted. It certainly will accelerate a healing if this principle is actually understood and applied.

How Angels Impact My Life

Part II

Rescue

How Angels Impact My Life

Life can be magical. Dramatic and unexpected rescues are prime examples of something tangible occurring that is beyond the mental and physical embodiment. To actively participate in the magical, I usually suggest to those who ask to be responsible for their thoughts, words and actions. Faith increases our vibration. Meditation, deep thought, unity and a desire for a greater awareness of the goodness and beauty that created us definitely raises our vibrational energy.

Understanding comes from firsthand experiences. Service, simple or more intense meditations expand the mind and soul. Authentic love and a genuine sense of brotherhood are a must. Although it appears that many people are shortsighted, and for the most part, have lost the awareness that is rightfully theirs, there are millions of us ready to step forward in faith through our desire to understand the Creator's plan, receive and live it. We are free-will creatures. Why not give up the illusion and allow our self to be easily healed, experience the outrageous, and actually live as a conscious and magical being?

An Early Angel Experience...

When my back was turned, our infant son crawled out into the upstairs hallway of our Colonial house. I was in the bedroom and heard a thump, thump, thump of something falling down the long stairway. It was the baby.

Shocked, I called the angels. Immediately, an invisible force lifted him into the air and held him there until I went down the necessary steps to scoop the crying child into my arms. Unbelievably, he was okay.

Angels have saved my life multiple times. They also at times convey assurance, bring specific guidance, healing and more. Their appearance can be radiant, large, small, or looking like a human.

A good example of a human appearance is when a friend of mine was driving her friends on a remote road and they experienced a serious car issue. A man appeared next to her stalled car and offered to fix it, which he quickly did. When she turned toward the car seat to get her purse to pay him something for his kindness, he was gone. This was an isolated spot with no other cars. The ladies thought they were alone and stranded. Here again, an angel knew and assisted in a very creative way.

Angels on Skis

My youngest son, ten at the time, and I decided to go cross-country skiing although the weather prediction for the day was dire. We set off in the woods that did not have a path with markers. We had traveled several miles and the predicted snowstorm began to quickly engulf us. Without a marked path, matches, or a flashlight, we struggled onward not knowing where we actually were. It became quite cold and nightfall was quickly changing our view. Tired, lost, and frankly worried, I suggested that we pray. We did not have a clue to our location or what direction to face.

I do want to mention that we never saw another person the entire afternoon. The area was obviously not a normal route for cross-country skiing. Immediately after our call to the angels, two people, a man and a woman, appeared on skis a good distance from us. They did not speak, only waved to us to follow them, which we gratefully did. It was so cold, we were tired, and I actually fell at one point. The angels patiently stopped and waited until we could continue to follow them. They never said a word.

After what felt like a very long time, I finally recognized the area we had reached. I called out, "I know where we are!" Our guides immediately vanished. As my son and I continued back to the vacant shack and the parking lot where my car was parked, there were no other cars in the lot or people to be seen anywhere. A side note: I returned the next day to the woods, went into the shack, and told the woman how we had been lost, not about the angels. As a result, she said she would suggest to the city that they place markers at strategic places and create a trail for the safety of future skiers. Not everyone may think of calling on angels.

Car

This is so outrageous, yet it is true. I was driving alone on the toll way in the farthest left hand lane. Everyone was averaging 70 miles an hour. A sleet storm suddenly occurred and the visibility was awful. I went to turn on the windshield wiper but mistakenly turned the water on to clean the window and it immediately froze. First of all, I had never driven to the destination before, everyone was speeding and now with a frozen window I was driving blindly. I couldn't change position. To make it worse, I did not know where the exit was or how far I yet had to drive.

I called for celestial help because it was certainly death for myself and probably others in this horrific situation where I was totally trapped. In the blink of an eye, I experienced what it would be like to be in a scene from a futuristic science fiction story. I instantly found myself at the top of an exit ramp, which led from a right lane. My car was in the correct position to make a left-hand turn on the road that led directly to my destination. What an outstanding display of power! Can you imagine the shock in finding myself in the car transported from the fourth outer lane of a highway to the top of a right-hand exit where I was safe in less time than it takes to inhale a breath?

Humanly, I did nothing. No steering or maneuvering of the moving car. I couldn't see at all because the windshield was iced over. I did get out of my car and scrape off the ice so I could see for the rest of my journey. The angels must have dematerialized the car and immediately materialized it at the correct and safe location. This still blows my mind in both wonder and gratitude.

The day I wrote the preceding story a friend contacted me and told me what she had experienced that very afternoon a similar car emergency. She was really in trouble driving this particular day. There were so many accidents and road closures; it took double the time to drive to her daughter's flat. The other passenger in the car did not drive, so he could be of no help. My friend could hardly see and knew she had to get to her destination that particular day. She was exhausted and could not concentrate. It was then that she asked the archangels Raphael and Michael to come to her aid. She could not see anymore and definitely did not want to get into an accident. Immediately, her vision cleared and the mind was alert. She was so grateful. Previously, she would not have thought about asking for something like this, but she did in faith and look how quickly love responded.

Drowning

I was on Lake Michigan in my friend's small sailboat enjoying the ride when a sudden storm came up. He said he must get back to the harbor to secure his sailboat. Then we needed to get into his dinghy immediately for our safety and get on land to prevent drowning. The sky was dark and ominous. Once we reached the dinghy, he urged me to quickly step into it while he took down the sails. If you have long legs, are a good swimmer and an experienced sailor, it would not be such a serious challenge. For me, it was.

The waves were high and tumultuous. I made several attempts to step into the safety of the dinghy and failed. The boats kept separating, and there was no way for me to jump from one into the other. Unexpectedly, and in a blink of an eye, an invisible force actually lifted me off of the sailboat and gently placed my body on a flat seat in the anchored dinghy. I was stunned and very relieved. I looked around to see if anyone had seen the miracle I had just experienced. No one was near. My companion was behind the sail still fussing and did not see my teleportation adventure. Nor did I ever tell him. I was shown again how we are both watched and loved. Everything happened so quickly that I never officially 'called' or prayed for immediate help. They knew I was in serious trouble and took action. It is obvious in the time travel experiences I have had that time literally does not exist. If any one were to have witnessed this spectacle, it would have been just too much to comprehend. It is beyond human understanding to actually experience it.

Rejection of a Healing

Instead of offering gratitude and feeling, a love filled with relief, some people react very unexpectedly to a healing they have personally experienced. An elderly person, a friend of a friend, contacted me by phone. One of her arms became useless after suffering a stroke.

After our remote treatment, the arm became strong and useful. A couple weeks later to my astonishment, the woman called and complained about her husband and she no longer wanted her dramatic healing.

She finally said that the only time her husband was good to her was when she was handicapped. He was actually thoughtful during her stress. Now that she could again do everything herself, the husband reverted to his previous unpleasant habits ridiculing and making life miserable for her. The senior decided that the ongoing criticism wasn't worth being healed and her being self-sufficient. She felt that he would be nicer if she was disabled and he had control of her life. Unbelievable that someone would make such a choice, but true!

Yes, there are dear souls who allow themselves to be weak and limited because they desire attention or release from responsibilities or simply wish to soften a harsh situation. Personalities are in control, and it is truly sad the nastiness many people will tolerate to maintain some kind of peace in their lives.

Rescued from Guilt

A father brought his daughter in a wheelchair over to our home for a healing. She had Multiple Sclerosis. I called the angels and she was healed within perhaps twenty minutes. As a result, she walked out of our home as her father pushed the empty wheelchair. Several weeks later, the girl called me and asked if she could come over to our home and I remove the healing. Stunned, I agreed. Once we met up again I asked, "Why?" She said she felt guilty because she was having sex with her boyfriend and did not feel worthy.

People never cease to amaze me. You probably would not believe a good half of the real-life stories I could tell. So much of what happens to us is the direct result of the 'mind' games we play. I am convinced that we are the ones who determine whether we are healed or not healed.

Rescued from a Disability

A mother of a child in kindergarten was burdened with multiple sclerosis. She already was having difficulty caring for her daughter and I could not help but wonder how she was going to function in the future. One day, I casually mentioned to her the 'gift' of healing and working consciously with the angels that I received when I was forty years old and had surrendered my life to God. She was surprised by my admission, because normally I do not bring up personal things about myself. We made an appointment to meet when her daughter was in school.

Usually, the process is very simple and I prefer not to speak. I silently call on the angels, which I did in this case. The young mother noticed a difference in her body that very evening. As the days passed, she was able to participate in more physical activities such as bowling with her husband and friends.

What I found amusing was the husband calling me one day and profusely thanking me for helping his wife. He shyly mentioned before closing the conversation that his wife was now even enjoying sex. That was the first time for me to hear such an admission.

Time passed and one day, I received a phone call from his wife. Her voice sounded strained as she told me she had a problem and wanted the healing removed. Again, I was shocked. It turns out that she was receiving monthly disability checks and in good conscience, she could not continue to collect them if she were healed. That made sense to me but why be concerned when her husband had an excellent job. Her answer was…are you ready? Although her daughter was five years old, the mother was depositing the disability checks in a special saving account for her daughter's future college tuition.

College tuition is high, yes, but to give up a healthy body for cash was beyond my understanding. Since what we hold strongly in the mind will manifest, her crippling disease gradually returned. I didn't have contact with her until the following Christmas when I received a greeting card. I could barely read her writing. It was all over the place. People continue to surprise and often dismay me. It is time for more of us to step out of our shell and spread our wings.

There are many forms of rescues. One of them is being rescued from a crippling and inconvenient situation. Consciously the desire may be there but on a deeper level, something else is in control. There are people who have a difficult time letting go of memories, particularly abuse. They can carry the memories for many years. They carry that anger around in them and it weighs them down. It can actually be a subtle influence hidden in the subconscious that they are not ready to let go of it. Finally, they decide that they are worthy and deserve a healing. In other words, the mother who chose to give up her healing so she could continue to receive a monthly disability payment might be fooling herself by believing that is the true reason she needs to be a cripple. The truth could be something very different.

Rescued from a Demon

A few years ago, a man came to me for healing help on his hip. Moving my hands over his body, a rather startling thing occurred. Seven of us had just finished our group meditation and the idea of an earth-bound entity speaking to us was the last thing we expected. My 'patient' began to address me in a very gruff and condescending voice. The strange voice announced that he was a pawn of Beelzebub. (I was not familiar with this energy.) The intruder attached to the patient's energy field claimed that I was wasting my time trying to heal the hip and that I had no power over him.

Not experiencing fear, I asked the entity how long he had been attached to the patient. The surprising answer was for a long time. He went on to say that, the man's pain and suffering increased his own power. I asked the intruder, "Do you remember any time when you were not in darkness?" He proudly answered, "I am a pawn of Beelzebub and cannot remember anything except what I feel at the moment." He again announced that he did not believe in the Light, also stating that love is nonexistent. According to the snarling voice, we were the ones deluded. He flatly stated the intent of all pawns of Beelzebub of watching and waiting for humans to become depressed, angry, resentful, weak and fearful. When we abuse our minds and bodies, we become easy prey for their manipulation.

I began to share at length with him about the unconditional love of God, which he claimed was nonexistent. Since I recognize only One Power and have been successfully guided through previous healing experiences, I told him that the Power of the Word was with me. I chose to flood him with love. The other people in the room willingly participated. Together, we directed love and the color pink to this invisible entity. He was removed from our friend's hip.

One of our clairvoyant friends saw the entity and watched his appearance change from darkness to Light as the group projected unconditional love toward the pawn of Beelzebub. A feeling of gratitude swept over our group. Everyone was reminded as to how we have a choice and create our own reality. I told the intruder that he also had a choice. He could follow the Light, having experienced unconditional love, or he could return to the darkness.

While still with us, I asked the entity whether he could come back and repossess our friend or another weak-willed person. Yes, was his answer. Other pawns, earthbound entities, can easily attach or possess a human if their guard is let down and they forget about the soul, cause harm, and ignore the divine purpose of life.

The intruder was healed and chose the way of the Light. How do we know that? We observed the change in his energy and the angels who came to support him. What about you? Remember to hold your shield high and carry the sword of truth with pure intent. Forgive yourself for past weaknesses and ensure that you remain strong now and into the future.

Further Comments

There are many forms of rescues. One of them is being rescued from a crippling and inconvenient situation. The most intricate and vitally important is the need to be rescued from our lack of understanding in the area of what we actually are and have forgotten.

How many humans genuinely grasp the significance of life and what they were prior to entering a physical body? The same holds true regarding what happens to us when we discard the physical body. The soul usually forgets its true self while in dense matter. There are always the few blessed ones who begin to experience a recall early in life and it makes all the difference in the world. When we understand that we are far grander than the temporary body of flesh we are wearing, it becomes a huge challenge. We become the exception. Being the exception is good, because part of the natural consciousness is not to cause any harm and to feel and understand the oneness of all life regardless if seen or unseen.

More of us need to be aware of our thoughts and words and the power they have. Example: If we believe absolutely that we can do a certain thing, the way will be open for us to do it. If we believe a lot of time needs to elapse, then that will be our experience. There is only One Power but, we use it according to our belief.

The subject of healing is of great importance. We have the power to heal ourselves and to help others heal. Our ability to do this will depend entirely upon our ability to see perfection mentally. We really have to watch our thoughts, because if we visualize the perfection for a few minutes and then start worrying and doubting, the healing is not going to work.

A suggestion that needs to be taken seriously: If you want to heal, stop seeing, reading about, discussing, or listening to conversation about sickness. You cannot do both—focus on the negative and expect to heal at the same time.

We reflect what we are. In other words, drop everything from your mind that contradicts your desire. Guilt is a huge part of ongoing suffering. Do your best to understand its insidious consequences. Words and actions that are harmful stem from the temporary personality, a personality that is not in balance. It is not your true and higher spiritual soul, the radiant part of you who never judges. God, Source, the Oneness does not judge. The only ones who judge are those who have not yet awakened and achieved the heights of a masterful consciousness. I'm not referring to discernment. Discernment sees clearly and naturally understands the source of dysfunction.

Possibilities

Guilt, fear and illness are related whether we are consciously aware of our feelings or they are lingering secretly in the subconscious part of the mind. Although we may call on the angels, they are not always able to assist if we have very strong feelings breeding within that we will not acknowledge.

Many of us here on earth at this time chose to be born because we wanted to create something here that will help others' souls. Wouldn't you love to make a difference and actually do something tangible to help nature, animal and life? But, for some unknown reason, we do not or not in the way that we really would like to. We were born with a bigger purpose in mind and we are not fulfilling our heart's desire.

The subconscious is so tricky that it can prevent us from doing what is required to fulfill our mission. Yet, it can be our best friend, because it genuinely has our interests at heart. We can have all the tools to be successful, but something is holding us back. Usually, it is one of the feelings already mentioned, guilt, fear or an illness. Guess who created the illness? If for some reason or another we feel we may expose ourselves to danger, we will find a way not to move forward with our original intention. Some people, not consciously, stall their purpose by developing a problem or illness.

We can be at the point in consciousness where there is no danger, there are people who want to help us and we have learned to love others without judgment and we still are not doing what we had planned to do. Now what is nonsense but yet truth is the fact that we can mentally create a disturbance in the physical body as a good example to keep us from moving forward. The bladder, the productive organs, or anything else in the body can become dysfunctional as a means to hold us back from our mission and other things involved on a more superficial level. When we hold onto things of the past, things we could let go of at any time, it definitely keeps us from accomplishing our dreams. The emotional junk we have accumulated can cause trouble in the body. Life is a mind game. Shocking but true, we create impediments to keep us from fulfilling or beginning our purpose. If we accept this truth and begin running divine healing energy, the white light energy, through our mind, body and emotions, we can energetically realign everything and function 100 percent perfectly.

You are worthy of loving yourself. The angels love you. You are Divine. Be responsible, help yourself, and make it easier for the angels to help. If you want to go more deeply into the healing subject, check out my other published books.

How Angels Impact My Life

Part III

The Unexpected

How Angels Impact My Life

There are angels and other unseen beings in the higher frequencies that enjoy helping us in time of need. There are no rigid rules. Angels help when we ask regardless of the challenge that confronts us.

They definitely will make 'the crooked places straight' if we ask in faith and have trust. Help comes in many forms, not only healing or saving a life. Angels can lead us to a book, an Internet connection, or an individual who can shed light on a challenge in a way that is very beneficial, and endless other possibilities.

We are so very grateful for the angels who send healing energy, a form of love, that they delight in sharing with Earth beings. Although help from the other side is wonderful, do not solely depend on it. You may fall into the habit where you become so immersed in relying on other entities / intelligences assisting, that disempowerment of your own spiritual strength and talents may occur. The One Power and Presence will flow through you if you have prepared the way for Its love. We, too, through our love, patience, application and trust may also become angelic right here on Earth in our physical bodies.

What has helped me when something unpleasant occurs in my personal life is to look at it as a non-reality. I don't mean to be oblivious, in denial, but look at the situation or individual from a higher perspective. It begins with understanding and accepting that we are actors in an ongoing drama, a play of consciousness. Behind this drama and the physical bodies or costumes we are temporarily wearing is God, One Power and the Holy Spirit. Holy Spirit is the creative energy. The greater our attunement with the Divine and our choosing to live in accordance with Divine Law, our path becomes easier.

Our real supply comes from Source. There are angelic helpers who we can call on to help when a challenge occurs. When our intent is to be compassionate, understanding and nonjudgmental, life does unfold like the many petal rose. Love, service and our faith create a huge difference compared to the common reactions toward human behavior and situations. The right people, things and circumstances are drawn to those who give of themselves selflessly to others. It is vital that we also honor our mind and body by keeping it filled with the beautiful and the good.

As a result of a close relationship with the Divine, truth is given to us through heightened understanding, glorious feelings, sights and sounds and an awareness that demands truth, kindness and a brotherly feeling toward all. When we consciously seek the Divine within, our inner teacher provides. Part of the provision are the guardian angels, angels and archangels. As the universe continues to unfold, so do we. The reality of God, the intimate touch of your own spiritual identity and angelic help are present.

You are a magical being. All of us are on a journey of awareness, which from time to time is momentarily interrupted by extraneous forces. Train yourself to perceive. Allow your heart and mind to accept that you are a magical being. Validity is established through first-hand experience. You have incredible resources that are waiting for you to use. Before I share some of the other unexpected angel interventions, I would like to share with you one of my favorite visions.

One evening while in a meditative state, I watched two life-sized butterfly-shaped forms appear as light-energy waltzing a dance of love. Their color was deep blue, the color of Spirit. I interpreted the energy as harmony, attained between the masculine and feminine principles. Another way to say it is the balance between reason and love. The goal is for us to be like the radiant and free spirit energy butterflies that appeared to me in the size of grown humans. When we awaken to the magnificence of our own God nature, we, too, can dance and soar the heavens as we are destined to do.

A Voice

Periodically throughout life I have heard a Voice carrying a message. It usually happens when I least expect it. It is loud and clear and the message certainly catches my attention. Angels will use this method of communication to get our immediate reaction. I have chosen this particular story because it was a different twist on offering advice from a celestial source when not even asked for.

One afternoon alone in the house, I heard an angelic voice say, "Athena." I was flashed instructions as to what I was urged to do. Some people might assume when hearing a name that somehow its ego and self-created. No, and I knew better. Perhaps, you will laugh at the following...I later laughed at myself. A visual was given me to visit a resale shop on the other side of town. I did not need anything from a resale shop, but being fascinated and obedient, I decided to drive over there and find out what was the point of the name 'Athena' being so clearly said to me.

I quickly went through the shop and didn't see anything significant until I was ready to walk out the door. Out of the corner of my eye, I saw on a shelf over to my left a large white bust of a woman. I immediately saw the name 'Athena' printed at its base! How the heck did an angel know what was on a shelf in a resale shop to prove a point and impress me? The bust was approximately sixteen inches high and a foot across. I was so shocked that I fled the store and drove quickly home. Once home, I faced the fact that there had to be a reason for this craziness. I returned to the store and purchased the bust.

Of course, the next step was to do research and find out why the message was given to me. Athena is an archetype. She was known for her winning strategies and practical solutions. I interpreted the symbolism as a suggestion that I must keep centered in the heat of emotional situations. Engage in logical thinking and according to the angels I could benefit from a more positive image of myself. So many of us who deeply care about life tend to not honor our own needs. The more I studied what Athena's energy represented, I realized moderation was necessary and a calm assessment of situations and people.

It is important to learn to think through things and be responsible and at the same time remember the symbolism of Athena's golden armor, a fitting symbol for ongoing protection. Angels obviously love and care for us. This is very comforting to know and accept.

I mention this particular story because it is not something I could possibly make up, but the angels with their discretion know what we will pay attention to and hopefully act upon. Athena is a goddess of wisdom and war. Well, surviving in life's ongoing dramas certainly feels like we are at war at times and we definitely will benefit by gaining wisdom. Also, don't think for a moment I mastered being calm in any situation overnight. It took many experiences to learn a genuine detachment, yet feeling compassion simultaneously.

Archangel Michael

Although we commonly think of angels as gentle, they can be quite fierce. One time, I had a negative energy follow me home from someone's office. I knew it was up to no good. Being sympathetic, I prayed calmly.

Evidently, Archangel Michael felt differently about the intruder. Suddenly Michael appeared unexpectedly flashing his sword swooping across the room where I was and removed the nasty entity. The powerful action was sudden and cleared the energy instantly.

I did call the owner of the massage office because I felt she needed to know what I experienced within the confines of her healing environment. Instead of healing, I experienced such a nasty reaction to her place that I looked into a mirror to see if I was really me. That is not a good sign.

It turns out her husband, who she was in the process of divorcing, was half owner of the business and he had just left previous to my appointment. They had been arguing and the atmosphere was so thick with his anger and the negative energy between them that it made me feel terrible. Now, the reason I am mentioning this part, is to share something else about Archangel Michael that I didn't realize until recently. Although most of us associate him with great drama such as the blue sword I witnessed flying across my bedroom, he serves in another capacity. Archangel Michael sees that guilt is often interfering with the happiness we seek. We blame ourselves more than we consciously realize. We need to let go of the past to be productive and healthy. Self-blame destroys our sense of peace.

Getting back to my dramatically nasty reaction to the massage experience to close this story. I had just spent a few weeks heavily involved with the sudden death of my mother and handling all her affairs. I had no one to help plus I had all my personal responsibilities still to take care of. What I did not do is honor me. When we don't take the time to take good care of ourselves, nasty things happen. I know many of us believe we must serve, serve and serve, but we defeat our purpose when we neglect our welfare.

Comfort

Angel experiences are not always dramatic. Sometimes, their appearance is simply a gesture of comfort and care. As an example, all of us have our moments of sadness and feeling very alone. I remember two times I felt this way. One was a bout of loneliness I was experiencing because of a loss of a very dear companion. I thought that perhaps going to a movie might lift my mood. As I was sitting alone in the darkened theater, I felt a presence take my right hand holding it gently. I was not alone, but very much loved! With a feeling of deep gratitude, my energy lifted and I felt whole again.

Because I have always had a natural and conscious connection to the angelic world of light and love, it is very rare for me to feel alone or sad. Another unusual experience was the loss of basically everything material in my life. I remember sitting on the edge of my bed feeling so very isolated. All of a sudden, I felt an invisible hand on my head. The hand remained until I felt at peace again.

Assistance

Sometimes, the angels help in very simple and practical ways. Our family was staying in a vacation cabin on a high, unlit, and rough terrain hill in Wisconsin. One night, we left our 'tree house' to join other campers in the valley below for a social activity. When it was time to return to our cabin, it was very dark and no electricity to light the upward climb on a dirt path. The return walk was a challenge, because we had not thought to carry a flashlight.

As the three of us were struggling up the hill in total darkness, I was thinking how nice it would be if I could actually see where I was going. Immediately after the thought, the entire area became lit as if the noonday sun was shining full force. The landscape looked like ethereal waves of light. I clearly saw everything and everyone. Excitedly, I asked the children, 'Do you see the Light?' No one had. For the time required to climb the steep path to the cabin, the opaque veil of illusion covering limited sight was removed and another brighter reality was exposed. The angels had shown their presence and love by turning on the etheric Light of God for a safe return to the cabin.

Repairs

I have had some very unexpected and strange help from angels regarding repair work in my home. One 'out of this world' example was when a dining room ceiling fixture needed to be repaired. A neighbor offered to fix the problem, but instead made an explosive mistake and caused the electricity and heat in half of our home to shut off.

My neighbor called a friend to help him solve the damage. They dismantled the circuit breaker as a last resort and did everything they could but to no avail. Then, they said they were going to the hardware store to buy new parts. When they returned, the new parts did not work. Frustrated and embarrassed, they said they were going to lunch.

In the meantime, it was February and very cold in the house as a result of no furnace working. It was also getting late and evening was fast approaching. I was not happy with a cold house minus electricity. I decided to take advantage of their absence and walked over to the fuse box. Using the fuse box as a focus point, I called the angels. I am well aware that everything seen and unseen is energy. I do have a strong connection and confidence in angelic help. I called and the angels responded.

Remember, it is done unto us as we believe. I definitely believe. The furnace and light suddenly came on. By the time the two volunteers returned with another man, an electrician, the house was warm and comfortable and all the lights on. The three men were stunned beyond belief and expressed fear. One of them kept saying, "You must have ghosts in the house." What an amazing experience of a practical form of love that was a blessing in so many wonderful ways.

Angels and Computers

It never ceases to amaze me how angels help in so many different capacities some of which have absolutely nothing to do with how humans typically look at Heaven or angelic beings. A few years ago, while writing on the computer, my keyboard would not function correctly. I could not type in lower case letters and part of the keyboard would not function. The left button when touched would delete everything on the page. When I would highlight one document in my folder, all documents would be highlighted. To my horror, the files automatically scrolled fast-forward and not one of the documents could be opened. The system tool restore function would not work. In the computer's

Word program, I could not type in a file name. The Word program was totally disassembled, incorrect. I called a professional and he could not help.

I did all I could. Since the angels have repaired other issues in and out of our home, I called on them. They are always close by. I placed my hands over the computer and asked that everything be corrected. In less than a minute, all functions were normal. I mentioned the experience to one of my children who lives out of state. Her reply was interesting. She said. "My computer at work experienced problems similar to yours and the computer technicians had a hard time fixing it. It took numerous tries over several weeks to get it fixed. It would work and then revert back to the old ways. It was a failure in the software." In my situation, real Power, angelic assistance, permanently fixed the computer.

A Different Reality

My dad in his senior years went through a triple by-pass surgery. During his recuperation, he experienced the presence of angelic beings in another form who he called 'Little People.' He claimed that the 'Little People,' who only he could see, devotedly 'worked' on the healing of his incisions while lying in the hospital bed. Doctors were both surprised and pleased by his quick recovery.

Later, at home, dad had an experience where he felt dizzy while walking in his room. He slumped back onto his bed. Feeling sorry and discouraged, an unexpected and sudden angelic presence appeared. The angel gave him a scene to view. He saw a very ragged, poorly dressed, dirty, skinny, pale barefoot young boy. The celestial voice said to him, "This is how you see yourself. Now, you will see yourself from a new perspective." The first scene disappeared and a new scene appeared that was dramatically different. Dad was shown as a well-dressed, handsome, clean, healthy and joyous looking man. The angel continued and said, "This is the real you."

Negativity

Anything is possible. One possibility that humans rarely think about is that negative entities in non-physical worlds can cause a human to become sick and die. A young woman was brought to our home that actually smelled of death. She was anorexic. My friend held on to her very carefully as she gently helped her settle down into a comfortable chair. As I stood over her, I became aware of an unseen presence that actually was her former sister who had died the year before. I intuitively knew that the sister had also been anorexic. The 'dead' sister was attempting to influence the living sister to stop eating and join her on the other side. Until that moment, the plan had been working. I lectured the 'departed' sister about moral issues and that it was time for her to leave the sister alone and move forward into a new life for herself in a finer dimension.

What I did next was to call on the angels to remove the lingering earthbound soul. They always help. The angels tool the sister to the next plane where she needed to go for a review of her life. Once the young physical woman became free of her deceased sister's influence, her health rapidly improved. The debilitating experience changed her consciousness in a very good way.

I find it interesting that science today is proving what many people in the natural healing field already understand. DNA itself is one of the carriers of consciousness. Our DNA holds secrets to consciousness. Experiments in DNA have shown that we have an energy body that emits photons. Photons are light. The power of the mind has the power to alter our DNA. This is additional proof that when a negative influence or negative thinking and feeling is removed, we can heal. As the result of her healing, the young woman decided to help not only her own balance, but also others. She enrolled in courses of study that would provide education and treatment for ongoing health, diet, and enhancing one's sense of self-esteem. It is a remarkable experience for me to work consciously with the angels.

The Future

It is very unusual for two people to experience a super conscious vision simultaneously. A friend and I were meditating in our living room. We witnessed great beings of wondrous light who lovingly gave approval to our mutual goal. We were conscious and alert as we were shown ourselves standing in the center of a large arena. The stadium was filled with white Light. The angels observing us were sitting in the bleachers and looked like living white flames.

Suddenly, we witnessed an immense transcendent purple Light as glorious vibrating energy. Beauty came to us as a garment of truth. The mutual vision lasted several minutes. We were not alone in our ideal nor are any of us. Angels and other forms of higher intelligence offer love and assistance to souls who believe and persistently put forth effort. Many worlds interface with one another. Angels live to serve God. Eventually, each of us will consciously reach the higher levels of purity and love and live it right here in matter.

The Subconscious

I remember asking the angels how I could help a friend who was immersed in self-abuse. I was shown an answer through a vision. The vision showed that the man in question had to walk down a flight of stairs to the basement. The basement was a total disaster. Clutter and garbage everywhere! It was up to him to clean the basement that represented his Subconscious.

What many people are not aware of is the fact that the Subconscious is our friend and desires to help us be whole. What I found fascinating is what the results would be if he actually chose to do the cleansing work. The next scene showed him sweeping the floor and right behind him was a being of Light in an identical form as him also sweeping.
In other words, once we make a conscious decision to be healed, the Subconscious, a reliable friend that has our best interests at heart, will pitch right in and help us as well. A drastic change as the result of a willing cooperation will

totally change the vibration in the Subconscious part of his mind. Did he choose to do it? No.

Visitors

Researching the following vision experience, I have not discovered any description that may explain the following manifestation that appeared to me unexpectedly during a Yoga class held in a friend's home.

I was doing the yoga movements with friends and suddenly I began to see Radiant Spiritual Light. I excused myself, because my visions some times last as long as 30 minutes. As I sat alone in the living room, a golden structure that looked like a chariot minus the horses or perhaps, a Sacred Merkaba slowly entered the room from the outside sky. Merkaba is an ancient symbol, a combination of three different words. Mer is a light that rotates within itself; Ka refers to the human spirit and Ba alludes to the physical human form. Egyptians believed that Merkaba is a rotating light that carries the human body and spirit from one plane to another.

Within the structure were three beings who I will call angels. They could have represented the power of three also mentioned in scriptural and non-scriptural texts. I was stunned, full of awe and when the other women came into where I was sitting on the floor watching this beauty, I stopped them. I was so overwhelmed by the majesty of what

I was viewing which they could not see, that I said please do not enter the room because something sacred was in process.

They respected my firm request and waited until I gave an all clear signal. I mention this as a reminder. Pay attention to the numbers, the symbols, the signs, etc. that repeatedly appear in meditation, prayer, dreams or when simply living your ordinary schedule. There is often a hidden message. For instance, the three visitors have been duplicated as the number three in multiple personal experiences reminding me of the purpose of my physical journey. You, too, may be experiencing similar messages.

Helpfulness

My youngest child and I decided we would go for a bike ride. Once we entered the garage, we realized that we could not. The night before unknown to us his dad had installed large ceiling hooks in the garage and hung our bikes upside down. As we stood there looking up at the ceiling disappointed, I placed my arms under my bike in the space between. In utter disbelief, my son and I watched the bike be lifted by invisible hands and slowly placed into mine as an angel very carefully turned the bike right side up and set it on the garage floor. The same miraculous procedure happened with his bike.

To be actively a part of such a demonstration is mind blowing. Humans exist in third dimensional density; angels exit in a much higher vibration. What we feel is impossible is a 'normal' activity in the higher dimensions. What a blessing!

Safety

This story is not as dramatic, but I am sure it saved my house from burning to the ground. I had set several eggs in a small pot to boil. I was getting ready to drive to a destination 45 minutes north of our condo. It wasn't until I reach my destination that I remembered that I had never turned the burner off. Boiling a couple of eggs usually takes 15 minutes at the very most.

I could not leave where I was for at least another half an hour, and then there was the 45 minute drive home. This time, I didn't take any chances. I called on the angels more than once to monitor the boiling water or possibly turn them off. No one I knew was around to check on things. Everybody was working and I had no recourse except to call for celestial assistance.

When I arrived home at the condo grounds, I was much relieved to see the building was not engulfed in flames and no fire trucks were present. I hurriedly rushed into the unit and ran to the kitchen. I was stunned! After about a 2 ½ hour span of time, there was still water in the small pot and the eggs were gently bouncing in about an inch or so of water. I have no idea how that feat was achieved. I am only deeply grateful.

Warning

Perhaps you have experienced a warning like I have about an impending possibility. Always listen and act on a message given. You could be saving your own life or someone else's. A good example was the time when I was shown my daughter doing her daily run in an isolated area amongst the beautiful trees.

The vision showed her being attacked and killed. My daughter lives in another state. I called her immediately describing what I had seen. She admitted to me that the tree-lined area where she ran alone was not frequented by others as a rule. She listened to my advice and found another place for her daily exercise.

The next day, a young woman running alone was attacked and killed in the very area that the vision showed it would happen. Thank God for the warning and the fact that my daughter listened and acted on what I shared with her. Her life was spared, but sadly the other girl's was not.

I have had multiple such warnings. I'm really sorry to say that all visions were not acted upon resulting in some very unpleasant results.

Human Angels

I could continue with more stories, but they can wait until another time. There is another genre of angels who are human and amazing in their own way. There are four human angels who made it possible for me to share this story with you. Carlos, a friend of only a year, came up with the idea of my making an audio book from one of my already published books. He was going to handle everything for me. Since I had never made an audio book and people have been suggesting I do, I gratefully accepted his generous offer. Instead of recording one of the existing books, I said that I wanted to create a new work of love using angels as the central characters. People need hope and love and to hear true stories that will inspire them during these challenging times. We agreed. His genuine interest in my ongoing journey of a higher love triggered something very wonderful.

I then called a very gifted poet/author/entrepreneur and asked if he would do the leg work on my new offering by creating an eBook and soft cover for me. He said he would as a gift. Bill is the managing director of Inner Child Press, Ltd., and is a profound and prolific poet and very talented.

Last and far from least, Rhonda, my beautiful, creative and sensitive daughter who edited my last book "Jesus the Ultimate Superhero." She also wrote a Foreword for the precious book. Rhonda immediately responded in the affirmative when I asked if she would proofread the "How Angels Impact My Life" manuscript.

My offering is the direct result of the combination of the above-mentioned human angels. There is a great need for messages of hope, healing and peace. Because of the great interest, I plan to write a sequel to this offering or perhaps, a series. I am forever grateful.

Surprise!!!

Before I close this part of my story, I would like to share with you something very dramatic that happened unexpectedly to me as I was rushing past a wall covered with a mirror in my home. Because the long mirrored wall was a fixture, a part of the house, I rarely looked in it. It was simply there. Well, one morning as I was rushing to leave for an appointment, something caught my attention and I quickly turned my head toward the mirror. I stopped suddenly because what I saw was unbelievable! I saw myself reflected in the mirror but with a huge difference! I had enormous wings extending from my back.

I know I am not an angel, so what did this appearance mean? After much thought, I came to the conclusion that it was a very dramatic reminder that we are never alone. There is celestial help, but we must ask for it. We often forget. The secret is to remember.

Why are some people not helped? It is because they must have something yet to learn about a particular issue. The issue can be anything. We need to learn to be responsible and be conscious about making the right choices for our welfare and those who are in need of care. Angels are for the times that we humanly are not fully equipped to handle a challenge for ourselves.

A Reminder

Life is similar to a giant puzzle. Many of us have at one time or another experienced the clairvoyant, seeing a large puzzle composed of Light. We have watched the various pieces slowly moving into place. It is time to fit everything together. Being cognizant of angelic help waiting to help us in time of need is an integral part to completing the puzzle.

The intention is to remember more and consciously connect with the subtle realms of Light and love. As we do, we will have more power to play joyfully in our earth embodiment. A strong part of our completing the puzzle is about allowing our angelic nature to open, allowing us to play. Being confident and relaxed, we attain more abilities to use involving the higher aspects of self.

The goal is to bring in the aspects or gifts of God that are whole and beautiful. As we consciously and willingly do this, we become alive with a heightened energy, an energy of Light. This allowing is celebrating a higher love by experiencing more of our previously suppressed god-like higher identity. It is about expanding and growing within the nature of God. In allowing our higher Self to more fully express, it will cause a sudden change in vibrational capacity. I am not referring to the power and presence only being with us in times of need, but all the time.

It is an energy that can be used for good and healing. You will be doing this not solely for Self, but for the good of all, the Whole. It is a movement within the Whole. A shift will occur from individual mind to wholeness and it will occur everywhere where it is possible.

Our willingness to do this is to be a conscious and active part of the vibration and frequency changes happening on Earth at this time.

Many are awakening now and being aware of their wholeness. All parts of the Source that were hidden or felt as if they were suspended, are now integrating.

Nothing is really separate. As more and more people merge with the whole parts of themselves, it makes it easier for others to accept. A good example is my life of daily visions, angelic experiences, and healing opportunities. Everyone could have this type of awareness.

Everything can and will eventually come together. More people will begin to realize they are not separate; they are one with the good, pure and beautiful and with all life. The goal is to more and more merge with the divine and whole parts of yourself. As we do, it will make it easier for others to accept. They will feel more comfortable with the idea that they are worthy and children of God.

We always have a choice. Why not choose to be connected to the part that is moving into wholeness. We may experience it without fully understanding it but don't worry, only enjoy it. It is integration and a lifting into a unified whole. More wholeness can function within each individual. Everything will feel more connected. The change happens primarily on inner levels.

How Angels Impact My Life

The energy is available to everybody and can be used in any way they want. An individual can decide whether they want to be part of it or not. When there is more wholeness present, creation happens automatically. Be careful what you ask for. Be careful what you want to create because it seems to be happening fast. Wholeness provides the answer to what you want. It is only when you do not know what you want that the creation becomes confused.

It is time to stop feeling guilt and suppressing feeling worthy of being happy. There is something beautiful going on where the angels and all the guides are starting to link. The linking involves knowingness, shared knowledge. The prime mover is always love. When you open more and more to your higher aspects, the mind opens up, the consciousness expands, and yes, you become consciously aware of more and more aspects of yourself and the loving angelic beings eager to help.

I am urging you to allow the trickle of Light to assist you in returning to a greater place, a greater knowingness, a greater beingness. There are many ready to be seeded with this truth. I do not share 49 years' worth of angels, healing experiences, miracles, visions and dreams to tout my blessedness. I share because this is your true nature as well as mine. Why not enjoy it? Souls usually forget once they enter a physical form, which is only meant to be a temporary garment. We do not have to forget or suffer or accept other people's opinions that we are not worthy and should feel guilt.

In truth, there is only Source. We see, feel, and hear negativity; true, but it is part of the dream and not a genuine reality. Stop allowing negativity to be absorbed into your consciousness and body. You are an extension of Light, of Source, of Wholeness, the One. And yet, you and most people stubbornly will not manifest that part of your created Self. You have Light so you can manifest your spiritual beingness. Open your mind and heart to your Higher Self and the amazing possibilities that you can personally experience. Allow the Light to fully enter. The world which we envision is already inside of us. We need to break fully out of our shell of confusion and ignorance. Say with me, "I am Light. I am Light. Hear me, God. I am Light." Come forth in your Light. Return to yourselves.

Stand tall. Break out of that shell. It is possible. Step out of the illusion we have created. The All cannot be altered. It is the humans who must deliberately accept that they have an inward perfection, but have temporarily forgotten. Go beyond limitation for there are no limits.

Progression is the key. To stand still is to become stagnant. Are you ready to fly? More of us need to get into our joy and know what we need to do, and when we tap into that joy, the magic is there. So, let us together move in that direction. Move, flow, and let ourselves heal and be complete. There is no limit.

Love,

Shi

How Angels Impact My Life

about the Author

Shirlee Hall, in the service of Divine Love, is a reverend, teacher, workshop leader, spiritual consultant, healing practitioner, public speaker and author of ten books. She views herself as a synthesizer, drawing the light, love, and wisdom of all ages together as a possibility right here in matter. She understands that the balance of love and wisdom, mind and heart is our redeeming quality.

Shirlee's primary focus is healing, including the body, mind, and soul. She strongly feels that if more people would understand their true worth as spirit in physical form, all levels of life will be touched and transformed. Based on personal experiences, her books offer love, hope, and peace.

Other works

by

Shirlee Hall

Jesus – *The Ultimate Superhero*,
2019, 176 pages, Paperback

Adventures in Consciousness –
Marvels – Mysteries – Miracles,
2018, 121 pages, Paperback and Kindle

Circle of Light Revisited,
2017, 209 pages, Paperback

Baba – *A Magical Cat with a message*,
2016, 114 pages, Paperback

Trapped: *Visitor from Heaven*,
2015, 194 pages, Paperback and Kindle

The Three Persuasions –
A tale for Inquisitive Souls,
2013, 32 pages, Paperback and Kindle

My Own Tree: *a healing experience*,
2010, 51 pages, Paperback

Be – *Embracing the Mystery*,
2007, 301 pages, Paperback, Hardcover and Kindle

Circle of Light,

1982, 183 pages, Paperback

Shirlee's Mission Statement

"It is time we become fully awakened and dance to the light of a higher melody that beckons us home to our spiritual Source."

Shirlee Hall's Web Links

www.behealedforever.com

www.facebook.com/shirleehallauthor

www.linkedin.com/in/behealedshirleehall

www.twitter.com/MamaShirlee

Inner Child Press

Inner Child Press is a publishing company founded and operated by writers. Our personal publishing experiences provide us an intimate understanding of the sometimes-daunting challenges writers, new and seasoned may face in the business of publishing and marketing their creative "Written Work".

For more information:

Inner Child Press

www.innerchildpress.com

intouch@innerchildpress.com

'building bridges of cultural understanding'

202 Wiltree Court, State College, Pennsylvania 16801

www.innerchildpress.com